Uncomfortable Ecologies

Elizabeth Joy Levinson

Attention schools and businesses: for discounted copies on large
orders, please contact the publisher directly.

For information contact:
Unsolicited Press
Portland, Oregon
www.unsolicitedpress.com
orders@unsolicitedpress.com
619-354-8005

Cover Image: Amanda Levinson
Cover Design: Kathryn Gerhardt
Editor: S.R. Stewart

ISBN: 978-1-956692-60-0

For all of my brothers and sisters
and the landscapes
we've traversed together
and apart.

Poems

By Land

Homebound

It's a fact. I can't do anything right   right now. My dreams are
about prostitutes, but when I'm awake, my teeth chip like old
wedding china in the dishwasher.

At night, when I flip the bathroom light, silverfish circle my
feet, seeking the cellulose and wheat paste, or flaked skin. My
skin flakes like so much old paint.

We are removing the layers with a putty knife or a chisel.
It is hard to know what walls will even be standing
when we are done.

I want daffodil walls, like the yellow-rumped warbler
that has visited our yard these past few days. That bright petal
tucked under his gray wings and bars.
Even the late April snow. Even though he is alone.
I need him to stay. If he stays, then maybe
I've done something right.
It is the only test I can focus on.
But warblers only migrate through, eventually he will leave.
And I will still not be able to.

Walk it back

Take one step back
and another
and another
until you can remember
what you gathered,
in each home
that wasn't quite there,
the trees always
held you closer.
Find the leaves
that brushed
against your towhead,
the rough boots
of the cabbage palm,
pull them back until
a small snake or tiny lizard
pauses in your hand.
Remember, they found warmth there.
Remember, your blood has not cooled.

Near miss

A small herd of deer
grazes the rough shoots
alongside the highway
and the sight of one slender neck
lowered and stretched to the ground
fills you with both tenderness
and dread.

You'd like to ask the driver
if you could stop
right here
and right now
but before you can even
give breath and shape
to the words
before you've even
completed the thought
the moment is gone
the distance increasing.

You consider your odds
even if you survive,
the deer will smell you before you will see them

and they will flee
perhaps back to the fields they came from
or perhaps into the rush of travelers
heading to the country
for the weekend.
If you leap,
even if you can still stand up,
even if you can still run,
no one will wait for you.

A horse is a door

after Magritte's Interpretation of Dreams

In the museum,
in a dream, a horse is a door, of course
in 1937 you probably could still ride
anywhere you wanted to go
but now, you'd need something else.

Right now, what I need is a field mouse
a downy gray and small, furry thing
a breakable thing
a warm thing
to place into your hand.

Let it run up your sleeve
and over your shoulders
and down your spine.
Don't move too much,
Don't lean against the wall
you could crush it or scare it
and while its nails make you shiver,
remember, it only wants

for some place safe
to curl up
and to sleep.

Like the memory
of your weight,
let it curl up in your ear,
like a warm secret:
as much as you want to keep it,
as much as it imbalances you.

Isopod

Lay plate upon plate,
sling this dream together
with thin connective tissue,
pull them tight,
round the robin into a ball,
let it fall into your hand
and look, in the slow slow unfurl uncurl,
can you see through?

What tiny heart skips a beat
before it opens,
and then,
what tiny legs
brush your flesh?

Home

Today I want to curl up inside
one of these Cornell boxes
to be the thing with feathers
or the facsimile of something other that,
even in paper, decoupage
could conjure the tickle, the soft chill
down your spine,
as you imagine
each twig carried swiftly,
each bit of thread
each patch of fur
held lightly in a hard beak
that could break open
the beetle's shell
or the banded case of an acorn
that could snap the neck
of a tiny mouse,
or crack the shell of another's egg
but doesn't, and instead,
tucks itself into your hand,
tiny beak tucked under wing.

Fur

It was bounding toward us,
form obscured in tall grass
until close up, we could see the misshapen body,
in fact, was two,
there was a second body,
      and you almost
      put your hands
       to my eyes.

This long-tailed weasel, running through the campsite,
holding tight to a likely still warm chipmunk,
and paused in front of us
      before leaping, finally,
     into the woods.

You told me not to look.
And I almost listened,
I almost missed it.
The loneliness of love
is that not one of us
will ever get it right,
no matter how hard we try.

This was no brutality,
this rarely seen thing,
a tawny sharp toothed thing,
and we both saw the same thing,
we both wear this memory,
a warm stole holding us together,
fur tickling our cheeks,
catching on our tongues.

Buttons

Under the bridge where objects collect
this bag of buttons exploded,
scattering red rosettes,
imitation tortoise shell,
drilled mother of pearl
caught the light from passing cars
cast prisms
across the muck
and concrete walls.

Lost from their original purpose,
had they memories,
those memories would lay
heavy in this corridor
some no doubt popped
by clumsy fingers
caught up in the cotton,
slipping on the plastic,
so desirous of what was beneath,
the soft breast
or mound of flesh and hair.
Others were perhaps lost
when the belly swelled

and forced the fabric to stretch,
and to stretch
as the skin stretched
around a new being,
in the process of becoming.
The threads could only bear
so much tension.

The way a seashell holds the ocean,
I want them to hold love.
I scoop the buttons from the ground,
I hold them to my ear
and I wait.

Exhibit A (a triptych)

I.
Hold close to the bur oak,
to the long and to the low
branches that beckon
what hairstreak?
what dusty wing?
The lilac orange, a bruise
resting on the bark.

II.
That the last of the first
should be the first of the last, should be
a silent heralding, full of leaf
of curled rain
snows in desert homes.
Once, in spring, we couldn't walk
without pink frogs underfoot
now only white noise, only
soft and even ground.

III.
Desperate as an orange grove
in an ice storm.

How beautiful anything
behind glass becomes
but unseen the cells expanding.
Crackshot of winter takes aim
and maims. The heartwood splinters.

We have nearly run out of helium

I am looking for summer tanagers
I know others saw them
of course, there is beauty everywhere
the sky is always beautiful, but
a flash of red feathers across it?

I am always scanning the trees
what discovery could be more than this?
I wish for a bird in my lungs, for
the power of song

But I am an accountant
I am measuring the sky for wingbeats
I will not sing, but I will wear
the drama of spring.

We have nearly run out of helium
I don't know what to do about flying.
Do I hold the bird in my hands?
Do I stretch my arms
and release?

Subnivean

Beneath feet of snow,
where it is less cold,
where small plants hold,
like studs, like girders,
walls built in sublimation,
tiny ice castles, crystalline rooms for
moles or mice,
they shelter in snow, until
sudden thaw and flood
an owl's talons,
the fox's keen leap and snout,
weaving ermine,
they haunt those halls,
and why shouldn't they,
which would you choose?

Hold this small velvet against your cheek
which softness does the world need,
which softness do we not?

This is a window strike

Indigo Bunting
break from my fingers,
the flight of you,
fraught and frightened,
frenetic energy
on fractured wing.

You won't get far,
the garden contains you.

To feel the beat of you,
how hard it is to hold you,
how hard to keep you still,
how hard it is to see you,
all refracted light,
crystallized- azurite, kyanite,
a hollow boned geode,
a trick of the human eye,
how hard it is to watch you like this,
but harder still
to look away.

Firefly

Japanese warriors
smashed them in their hands,
to read the maps
leading to enemy lands.

In Connecticut,
a good doctor
washes his
and gets to work.
A military grant
funds his research
to move beyond navigating,
to find ways
to manipulate
the cold light
so it is just beyond
human vision...

They want
to land helicopters with it,
to examine heart attack victims,
to develop security systems.

It is the end of summer, dusk.
I watch my nephews and my father
run through the yard
each with a mason jar in one hand
the lid in the other
until they come upon
those tiny flash bulbs,
one gets caught in the threads
as they capture it in haste,
blinking,
blinking,
fading.
It dies
behind glass
on the nightstand
as the boys
fall
to dreaming.

False Narrative

Again, the snow falls,
again, we all try
to capture the flakes
in pixels the way
the flakes catch the light,
 the way the city sparkles
under a blanket of white,
white and light.

What is it about a thing that sparkles?
what is it about a diamond,
about a row of sequins,
expertly stitched to a sliver of a dress,
or the mirrored ball hanging from the ceiling,
What is it about a crystal highball glass
with a bubble of air in the base?

Kids split mica sheets until it is a transparent film,
they try to chip the glitter out of a piece of granite.

We have imagined magpies
lining their nests with shining objects,
when really,

we just want to lay down
these tired bodies,
in the soft, cold snow,
let the drifts
cover our ashen faces,
and make us lovely again.

The Starlings of Bridgeport

Above the city that burned
and burned and was rebuilt with lights
that bounce off the atmosphere
and yellow the sky, casting out the stars,
the starlings rise.
With wings spread
they darken the night again,
and feathers, lit at the tips,
spark like dying embers.

They create constellations
and call out new compositions to each other.
No one understands why.
They have risen from the ashes
of a wild city that burned years ago
and were buried beneath foundations
of brick and concrete.
Every night, just before the city sleeps
the starlings call out
and a memory might respond.

Easement

There is something trying to live
everywhere, quietly
in the stubbled thyme
vining the cracks
in the mortar,
green rivers,
gristled leaves.
Brush your fingers against it,
gently, your hand
will be inhabited
tiny white flies,
a cricket nymph
spider mites
in scarlet constellations
across your palm.

But this is easy to imagine,
there are so many corners,
ecotones we'd rather ignore
where something is breathing
a spark of energy,
that might leave you wounded
were you to dig around
something is always struggling
beneath the rubble,
that wild square foot
between your home
and the alley.

You say one day, you'll
plant something there,
but you don't
you only dream about it,
a dream of lost teeth
that are not your own.

Parakeets in Douglas Park, Chicago

The monk parakeets cross over the trees,
like pears to wing,
like the green dreams of the leaves
that were all crushed
when they fell to the ground
under the feet of so many who pass through.

It is strange the parrots would stay as the wind stays
as the wind picks up strength. This was never a home for
      them.
but where else would they go?
removed from their homes and then released,
it is no freedom
to be so far from home,
yet, they weave sticks so strongly together,
they bend the power lines, pull down the poles
people lose electricity, fires start,
and nobody knows for sure
what the right thing is.

The Beekeepers

What makes them do it,
these strange men who love
a thing that is dying.

Each day they suit up,
like monks or astronauts,
mysterious as either.
They count the carcasses
each one so light.
Those that are left
beat furious wings,
a dead march
that moves the beekeepers
from hive to hive.

Each day they must decide
to divide the colonies,
rebuild
or sell them off —
there will always be those
who have not yet known

the bitter aftertaste
that follows
the harvest of the comb.

This is something I would like to try:
in a field of clover,
to watch them over,
to press the bellows
of a tin smoker
to wave it around
making gray clouds
to move in and out
pulling each tray
with hope for the quiet hum,
for the brush of a furry thorax
against my wrist,
where my gloves might slide down
leaving skin exposed.

She Fakes an Injury to Save Her Children.

The broken-winged display of a killdeer,
the feathers spread,
one wing open,
the red rust underlay shown,
she is loud,
she is in pain,

Never mind this is just what I said,
a display,

Whatever it is, it comes from a source
the nest is threatened,
the young are still immobile,
still vulnerable,
all puckery skin
and patchy down,
each small beak,
still wearing its egg tooth,
open wide,
letting out
those small naive cries

that only know the mother,
the father,
and not that anyone else
is listening.

Overtoun Bridge

The dogs leapt
No fear, but fever
Legs outstretched, ready

     and they fell   fifty feet
          they fell
               and only found their deaths.

What strange impulse
overwhelmed them?

To survive,
what must we come to ignore?

What foolish mink weaves
between our legs,
marking our ankles --
how quickly we reach down,
         how easily we tumble
           and find
the furry thing we sought
is gone.

You are where you are from.

Wade out through the fog
far past the house.
By the time you reach
the edge of the field
your hair will be damp,
it sticks to your face
and there's a cold finger
pressed against your lips.

Tell this secret
to the switchgrass that towers over you
gather the stems in your arms
their furry flowerheads
will brush the word
from your cheeks
like the hard, golden seeds
like the cells from your skin
it will lift with the mist
and leave you feeling forgotten.

Coyote

As wild as you are,
you won't step over the
tall grasses on the edge of the pavement
I listen for a leathery pad pressing
that dried and frosted ground --
crystals formed on blades of grass crackling
but it doesn't come.

The diseased trees, their branches down,
the brown leaves glassine with winter,
they are your barrier
and mine as well.

I know you are there,
feeling out the distance
from one side of this road
to the other.

 I dig a hard heel into the dirt
It gives easily and for a moment,
I am sinking.

Your snout dips, you swallow me in
and decide to turn back the way you came.
and for now, we have reached an accord,
but I'm wondering how long
before the brush is cleared away,
leaving you unveiled,
your hair bristling, standing on end.

Domicile

I'm feeling how the prairie
might have moved beneath me,
grasses with roots that grew deep
into the earth, so they could withstand
the often fire and
long winter.

What tender blades broke beneath these bricks?
Some days a home feels like less than that.

When I reach my hands into the soil,
to feel its sickness,

shards of glass, rusted nails,
what grows here now,

in these small carved out spaces,
between the homes and the roads,
it isn't from here,

it dies a little each year,
needs the constant reseeding,
needs constant,

constantly.

What you don't know

Frost forms shapes on the windows,
that house, there,
an old-fashioned wedding dress on display
the intricate lace would dissolve
under the warmth of a hand
a finger wiggling its way through
seeking the slightest peek
at the secret warmth
inside of you.

Transfusion

Down the street, the house
under the tracks
how dark it must be,
all the windows boarded over.
When the front door opens,
and I can see in,
how hard to imagine
that this was once a home

How cavernous it seems
and the men,
like miners
move expertly through
the building
they know where
to cut and rip,
following the veins
that used to flow
to the television,
the ac,
the light over
a dining room table,
who once sat there?

who once ate food in this room?
They pull whole handfuls through
the drywall and mud,
lengths and lengths of
corded energy.

It is an uncomfortable ecology,
when they come back out,
two women wait
with buckets and knives,
they slit the rubber sheathing,
shucking copper
from the sleeves,
hoping this thin conduit will
become something
viable again.

What wolves have you been?

What wolf are you? and what wolves have you been? the truck stop t-shirt with the wolves walking through your chest, the one you begged for when you were ten, what do they know of you, having been through your ribs, bones that cage nothing, not your lungs, which have always breathed evenly, but that's not how any of this works.

What wolf are you? graying against a gray sky, how long have you waited to eat? have you always waited to eat? when you were hungry and chewing saltines in the back of a minivan parked for some time, what were you even waiting for? water. you waited for water.

What wolves have you been? the sharp side gnash and nip at the small and vulnerable. when they fuck up, you will hurt them to save them, but you will also hurt them to save yourself. you didn't mean to, but you probably smacked a wrist. you were ten. what were you waiting for? the wolves were out hunting, but you stayed behind.

The Long Drive

Drive into those areas of crowfoot grass,
exploding hydrangeas,
trees with leaves thirty feet
in the air.
There's the earth smell -- musty, musky,
rotting pine, clean and damp
with decomposition.
Small homes there
are homes like no others
with chipped paint,
wrap-around porch stairs.

Drive into the flat moon nights
flat noon times. The heat
quiets everything but
the soft thrum of cicadas.

Pass red ants tunneling
around front lawn cemeteries,
around pine box coffins
old bones picked clean, white --

ghosts kept quiet,
families holding on and on
in those grandfathered burial grounds.

Insufficient Funds

I am sorry I have existed, taken up space, opened my mouth and spoken or opened my mouth and did not speak. I stepped on a butterfly. I stepped on a crack. I stepped on concrete. Someone put concrete down for me to step on. I bought a dress. I did not buy a dress. I did not make myself beautiful, with painted lips and laughter. I was unkind. I was a different kind. I was a stereotype. I was the kind of girl who could not hold her horses.

I begged for the horses. I left the horses in the pasture. I left the horses out in the rain. The horses were on an island and the shoreline was eroding.

I abandoned the land. I did not have enough boards. I did not bring enough nails. I left as my toes were getting wet.

I was a good daughter. I sent a check.

Everything

The white fingers
of the sycamores
reach out
against the cerulean sky,
the moon white and translucent,

Am I white and reaching and translucent?

I am white and reaching and translucent.
I am a killing frost at dawn
or an ice storm

I am trying
to hold everything
at once.

By Sea

Weighted.

I am filling my pockets with stones
that line the edge of the lake we walk along
on a stolen Sunday afternoon.

We should both be working,
our figures bent over screens
in separate corners of the cottage,
but even if it annoys us, even if
we resent each other a little,
we both agree.
To stop.
To walk barefoot.
The dog between us, barking
if one of us strays too far off course.
If only it were all that simple.

I am weighing myself down with the stones.
I try to name them as we turn them over.
The pink of feldspar rich granite,
green veins in the unakite,
the deep blood running through a banded jasper.

I want to ground myself in this moment,
already past tense, already memory.

I pull from the receding tide
a fossil soup full of tiny "O's"
like the eyes or mouths of ghosts.
Like the eyes or mouths of ghosts.

The portrait of an addict as the elements

The fire you set inside yourself,
you know you lit the match even

water is heavy, the way your body
is heavy, the way you just noticed
you can't lift your own arm, like
every muscle has water bags strapped
or every appendage is being pulled
by a rip current in an opposite direction.

The room is pulled until it is hard to recognize.
Walls buckle but the flame does not.
You cave into the earth, you wish
you could have caved
into your mother's arms but she was not
that kind of mother. She was as easy to hold onto
as air, maybe that's why you started smoking
at twelve, you wanted a mother you could hold onto,
you could hold air in your lungs, you could hold the smoke
until it became a part of you.

When we were children, we were mermaids.

In water, in snow, when we are tuck tired in a wet sleep,
in a saturated dream, these are my hands in the sink,
these are my feet in the ocean,
and I'm holding my breath,
with my lungs somewhere in between.
We were always under or in or maybe
just off to the side, intracoastal
water, wander, wanderer.
We needed only carry our bodies
through the waves,
enough that we were too tired to notice
all we left behind.
We were always swimming,
even when we were not, when we
were wrapped in towels,
laid out on the shore,
legs bound in cotton curls of terry cloth
too tired to remember
where we had come from and
where we were going to.

Florida Girl

Florida girl is eating a stalk of celery with peanut butter and sand. She is trying not to choke. Florida girl knows about flannel moth caterpillars and puss caterpillars, how soft they look and how dangerous their fur. Florida girl is always chasing her baby brother, who can hit a lizard with a rock dead, despite that he is only three and doesn't ever want to wear clothes. Florida girl has an illegal pet tortoise. Her father almost hit it and said it would have died. She feeds it lettuce and lawn. Florida girl has rich friends, which she shouldn't. They take her to amusement parks. Once, she lost twenty dollars at Busch Gardens and cried over it for weeks. Her Florida sister works at a bakery for less than minimum wage because she is less than minimum age and she brings home day old bread sometimes. Florida girl drinks orange juice from the oranges in the yard. Florida girl has sand in her food because she is always at the beach. When Florida girl's scholarship dries up, she transfers to public school, where she is bullied mercilessly. One day, in geography, she stands on a desk and yells "Leave me the fuck alone." And miraculously, they do, everyone, the teachers don't even call her parents. Florida girl wishes she had yelled anything else instead. Florida girl never has the right words. The Gulf of Mexico swallowed them all.

Things no one told my parents and, also, why I got a D in geography

Try understanding geography when
the map is always changing, when
the world is holding
a magnet to your compass,
the pin marking "you are here"
isn't a pin at all, but the silver ball
of a pinhead rolling around
to the sound of the ocean.

They were listening for the sound
of the ocean and maybe
they were listening
in all the wrong places.
A tin can can sound
like a conch if you want it to.
The conch is only an illusion anyway,
who is to say where
that magic comes from.

For me, it came from the car stereo,
ballads on breathing and rain
in smooth synth and well enunciated lyrics.

How easy to pretend
you were a song story
when there was no place
your story belonged.

No one told them how hard it is
to anchor anything to the ocean.
How easy to drag
until you don't recognize
the shoreline you end up on.

At The Party

The Gondolier in
brown polyester pants
and red and white bateau neck
moves across the floor
like the tracks
in his arms
are grooves
in the wood
he can slide through
jump over
pivot and return
and do it
all over
again.

Every poem is about my father

Is what I tell people at parties, when they ask.
It is as true to say as it is true to say
that every poem is an apology
or that every poem is an origin story.
They may be one in the same.
I am always using my father to excuse my own misbehaviors.
When I was a child, I kept things, a wild menagerie
of secret insects, salamanders, snakes, usually
they died before they could be released.
I was building a curio of guilt, so I would have walls
that lasted around me where the walls were so quickly
coming down, being rebuilt, changing shape,
we were ephemera in the world,
we moved so quickly,
I'm not sure if I was there or just a ghost,
a scale of a girl, now a fishwife,
I don't yet know how to live with people,
I think I have it down
and then I open my mouth.

The Fire-Eater

He learned the trick in the army,
where he spent two years
inspecting food and getting high —
mealworms swimming in sacks of flour,
they must have plagued
the dreams in his veins, but
this is the nature of his narrative,
no matter how many times I hear it,
it is difficult to knit these bones together,
to understand how he progresses
from one event to another,
are these the joints that haven't set right,
hands always cupped but empty?

Either way, there was always a motorcycle,
Japanese of some make
and he was in the German countryside
stoned out of his mind,
and he came upon a circus.

I hope he doesn't mind it,
but I imagine him surrounded
by sequined girls and clowns

and fire eaters
thrusting burning batons towards him
before extinguishing the flames in their own throats,
it was a trick he learned to perform,
one of many he used to keep us enthralled,
before we understood anything at all,
how basic a thing it is,
to deprive a fire of oxygen.

Leaving

In the back of the old station wagon,
one sister on each side of me
like strangers, they are to me
negotiating the room between
our legs stretched over suitcases,
our laps an array of toys, of books.

Amanda twists her lips, her eyes squint
for the benefit of other kids in other cars.

Rebecca sleeps, tired from so much riding
her legs are too long, they are growing everyday now
they are twisted at odd angles,
her lungs heave loudly, sucking down
the re-circulated air.

There is no novelty here.
We've done this before.
Because we are gypsies
or poor, or because my parents
see promise in everything--

my gaze sweeps over my sisters
but holds on the landscape.
On the edge of the street
the budding leaves
look different
everywhere we go.

Exterminator

In Florida,
you tried everything
but you couldn't kill the insects
faster than they could hatch
so you taught me about them instead.
I learned to identify
orb weavers
mole crickets.
I kept a close watch
when they came out
just before dawn
to drink
from condensation
on blades
of tangled crabgrass.

Those mornings,
I wove my toes
into the stubborn plant's runners,
grainy soil stuck to my skin.
as the sun heated up,

the smell of rotting oranges
so high in the gnarled tree,
we could never pick them all.

You moved on,
sold solar panels,
adjustable beds,
insurance. Roaches multiplied,
we could not keep up.

In the evenings, we rinsed in the ocean,
we were never clean,
never refreshed,
but we were tired,
we slumbered dreamlessly.

Eventually, all that wasn't living
sank into brown shag
behind white stucco walls
built on crawfish, cockroaches.
They scurried between our feet,
watching, as we fled, left our things:
plastic Legos, silverware, socks.
Hidden from us, much later
we realized they were gone.

We left those things and
the salt-heavy air
the way the moisture collected on skin,
with sweat and hot dog grease.

It was better that way,
to leave,
the ocean always burned
my thighs chafed inside
and eyes red

as the ink on the eviction slip
and the tongues of the lizards flicking
as they ran across the door.

Homecoming

After eight months at sea
he still hasn't found his land legs,
my father walks in feebly.

We must seem as mermaids,
more bitter than benevolent,
dragging him from his ship.

At dinner, he repeats himself,
a joke that no one hears,
every time, he gets a little louder.

When his feet take a more steady gait
I notice the way my mother's dress
catches the light when he spins her.
Does he see cheap lamé
or scales against her skin?

He has gone completely gray.
His hair is cut too short.
When he stands next to her,
he looks older than my mother.

Later, while dancing he says,
"You will only be able to have
 half the things you want in life."

He dips me, and for a moment,
I find myself pulling him down again
without even trying.

Hurricane

Gloria came in '85,
had us huddled
in the coatroom,
under a cloak
of wool and down,
the acridity of once living things
reduced to useful artifacts.

Everyone knows to
avoid anything glass, but
you took me out the french doors
in the eye of the storm,
the air charged and warm
it wasn't raining but
my skin felt damp
and the sky, the purple-yellow
of a new bruise.

Was this the first time I felt brave?
or the first time I felt defiant?
And I wonder
which of the two led you
to bring me through

holding tight to my hand,
as the wind picked up,
and took our laughter
from our lungs.

My Father's Hands

I damn my fingers, child-like digits
dry, a woman's skin older than mine.
They bleed easily, they split in the cold,
around the knuckles and the nails
where they are creased the most.

So soft
even knitting can sting,
even cashmere yarns
can chafe and leave me raw.

Your hands more calloused,
thick pads of dead skin built up on each tip
and you, always so impatient with me.

I could never hold the line,
never pull quickly enough.
It burned too much.

You sat me down
when I was five,
made me watch as you brought
right thumb to right forefinger

and stitched the two together, the black thread
a dead worm under your waxy flesh.
The snap when you pulled the thread
pulled tight my chest.

When you tied off, you looked at me,
your hand held together like a shadow rabbit,
you danced it around in front of me,
showing off your embroidery.

You laughed until I laughed, until you knew
that I knew you were okay.
I wanted hands like that.

My nephew leans his head into my hand.
His skin, like peach, like lamb's ear, the downy leaves
of mullein pink, but different, a slight nuance
you would not feel.
He says, "Papa sewed his fingers together,"
and he's agitated by the simple trick, concerned.

I stroke his forehead, ruffle his hair, explain
about calluses and how they form and why.
Today -- my hands as I wanted them to be --
today, my hands are mine.

Close

As children, we would find them
deflated sacks flat against the land.
Kicking up the Atlantic
brought moon jellies to the shore,
their tentacles already shriveling
rendered impotent
by the air and the sand.

Once, I drifted in those waters
over a grouper lounging
at the bottom of the ocean
his mouth gaped wide.
I still recall the taste
as I tried to get closer
and the water filled the snorkel
that was keeping me in air
I surfaced, choking and sputtering
and by the time I recovered, he was gone.

There is no way of knowing
how these memories may
weigh me down more
than any other.

Another time, I was bewildered.
Ten feet below me a green turtle swam,
his flippers waving, beckoning me closer,
but the current was strong and
threatened to rake me
over fire corals,
and I came so close
but there was a jelly,
it almost brushed my cheek
I lost sight of the turtle
as I righted myself in the water.
It was nothing.
Another day.

Broken Water

In the V-berth, I was re-birthed.
Every morning, I rose before my shipmates and
went above to watch the sun
appear in the horizon.

Throughout the day, I baked.
Sometimes small pustules formed on my skin,
pearly and taut,
tiny and smart, they broke away
when I brushed my hands over my arms
and felt that small relief of the water,
leaking out and spreading over me
before evaporating. We are all part sea.

Overcoming the tiller, learning the way the lady moved,
I was new. Each day, each different passing landscape,
I was new. Every time we came into port,
I liked to sound out my new language,
One hand on the life line, the other throwing out a rope,
and when I stepped off the boat,
I shook the hands that caught and tied me off safely.
Each time, they were new hands.

And in each port,
I tried new paces,
new swings, new words,
I was moving.

At night, I showered on the deck,
sun heated water in a bag
hanging on the mast.

My shipmates were two strangers
or, one was my father
the other, a lover.
It didn't really matter.
There was no way of knowing
that could have overcome:
the changes in the water
were predictable.

I was not.

The Wild Horses on Cumberland Island

In the morning, they greeted us,
grazing in the shade of the field house
at the dock.
They were not the pasture-fed
thoroughbreds of the Midwest,
their hides were pocked with scars
whorls of hair around sores or ticks,
thin manes twitched as flies circled the air
around their ears.
They were indifferent.
A stallion, two mares,
only the yearling paid any notice
as I left the boat and approached,
she tossed her head, nostrils flaring,
she pranced around the elders nervously,
and when they failed to react, she came
near to me. We were five feet apart,
and her sleek chestnut coat was still
unmarred by the elements.
She stepped closer; one, two
I was afraid to stay, I was afraid to move,
I was so worried about what would come next,
and I regret I can't remember

if her forelock was white,
if the hair hung in her eyes,
or if she quietly whinnied
as the stallion finally regarded me
with a snort of disgust
that called her back.

Shark's teeth

Last summer,
my hand was a sieve,
shifting through the sand for
the tiny sharp thing,
serrated angles against skin,
I made a game of every mistake:
a broken shell, a shattered crab's leg, a yet unsoftened piece
         of beach glass.

How each tooth drops out,
how one moves up to take its place,
row upon deadly row, now,
washed upon the shore,
as deadly as a splinter
or a thorn, and just as worthless, yet
I press a point against a fingertip
and my whole arm is devoured.

I sought to make a gift of them,
to rest my death inside your palm.
The time was swallowed in the searching.
Water in my eyes, the tide rolled over me.

Some Men Bring Flowers

The house I bought was in disrepair
the yard overgrown
nightshade and thistle almost as tall as I.
A marijuana plant,
lone, therefore useless
was hidden in the weeds.
When my father came
to help with the plumbing and electric
I pointed it out and he quickly cut a leaf from the plant
for my mother who, inspired by some TV show
has been thinking of starting
a medicinal marijuana farm.

My father wants to sail to Cuba,
he's making plans with a few other boaters
who have done it before.
He says, tell your mother nothing.

Months later, I visit them,
my father hasn't left yet,
my mother has hung
the nine-pointed leaf on the fridge
in a flat wax bag

its fingers dried and curled.
I imagine that if I took it out
it would crumble in my hand.

Emergency Procedures

He's got a hand on the tiller,
and his sights on the sea
and the strength in his arms
carries through the lines, up the mast
moving us forward
while my own legs
lock around the lazarette
and my thighs clench tighter every time
we keel, 15, 20 degrees, and when
I can almost reach the water,

he asks, *what would you do now
if something happened to me?*

and I do not cry while he explains
how to sail into the wind
how to bring the ship to a dead stop at sea
so I can take the main down before
seeing to the patient, before the *mayday...*

mayday, mayday

A loggerhead comes up for air, it is right beneath the surface,
and I point it out -- this is my protest.

In time, barnacles will build whole worlds
on the bottom of a boat abandoned at the township dock,
the captain landlocked, me and my sisters will argue
on the best way to care for him
and he will be so diminished. And we will be so wrong.

And I do not want to know this, that it will not be so easy
as finding the wind and sailing into it,
watching the canvas go slack
with little luffing,
with little fight.

Recovering

Some days he travels for hours
at best, makes seven knots
and sees no one.
The waters are charted,
but these edges of the Intracoastal,
too soft and too green.
Like the history of his veins,
they are murky.

In the waters
no one asks him to speak
no one tells him to stop talking
the dolphins don't care what he does,
they flank the sides of the boat,
they may stay with him for a while,
or not.

It's okay, alone
running aground,
the keel buried in silt.
He waits,
as the tide rises
he floats away.

When he passes through more solid territory
buildings take footing and floodlights
falsely pull creatures from the sea
shorelines take shape.

Forty years ago
there were nights on the beach
when he slept soundless as the sand
that stuck to his cheeks
but even here,
in slow currents
it continues to compel him.
Standing with the tiller between his legs
he gently shifts away.
Where he sees no one
neither is he seen.

Fossils in flagrante delicto

a poem for prehistoric turtles

Perhaps they knew what was coming,
felt light headed and giddy as tiny bubbles
broke at the surface,
releasing the poison pooling
deep, deep in the lake,
accumulating, waiting.

And just as we could, they
sought each other out, locking together
at the bases of their shells,
forming figure eights,
infinity never had a truer representation
this manifestation:
In the face of death,
life clings
to life

as they clung to each other,
sinking, sinking
the water becoming darker
around them, the swirling muck
and gasses growing thicker,

they did not disengage,
they did not fight each other,
one did not violently kick at the other,
pushing off and breaking for air,
but instead,

they held on
and fell.

Yes, the world is weary and
we are world weary in it.
but this is something so obvious to learn from,
we can struggle against each other
or we can entwine our bodies,
braided bones to be found years from now,
one fossil of not a being,
but an embrace.

Home

At 38, my younger sister has started collecting
olive shells, however many she can find, their lettered
and netted shapes litter her shelves, they spill out of plastic
boxes,
ziploc bags and mason jars.

How hard a thing it is, to hold onto a place, to say
I live here and I am of here. How does a person come to
belong?

I've rested the skull of a house sparrow in my attic office. Is
home
the place you bury your dead? (House sparrows are from
Europe. There, they are disappearing. Here they flourish,
 they outcompete.)

I have olive shells, too, their incoherent script like
electrocardiograms, but nothing lives inside anymore,
only the memory of the body
it once carried. And the memory of the bodies they carried
beneath the sand where they held their prey close,
until it was absorbed. I run my thumb over
the smooth outer lip, over the sharp edges
of the crowning spiral.

I ask my husband
if he knows what to do with me when I die?
Somewhere in this house, I have a garfish scale,

somewhere I have a butterfly
pinned up in a frame.

Las Grietas

(the cracks)

In the water, cold, clear,
the things we could hear
small shrimp or even smaller fish
a crackling chatter, a static whisper,
disappeared my own thoughts --
everything I needed, except air

When I lift my head above the surface,
sun, the sun, how hot it hurts
the jutting cliff walls look quick to cut
and how loud the crowd, waiting to dive in.

Acknowledgements

I am so grateful to all of the journals who published individual poems before they came together in this collection:

"Homecoming," *Apple Valley Review*, Spring 2010
"Beekeepers" *Grey Sparrow*, Summer 2011.
"She Fakes an Injury to Save Her Children" *Wild Times Out East*, Fall 2011.
"Recovering," *Hobble Creek Review*, Summer 2011
"Domicile," *Hawk and Whippoorwill*, Winter 2018
"The Wild Horses on Cumberland Island," *Alluvian*, Spring 2019
"Parakeets in Douglas Park, Chicago," *La Presa*, Spring, 2019

"Insufficient Funds," *Landlocked*, Summer 2019
"Exterminator," *Slipstream*, Fall 2019
"Broken Water," "Close," and "When we were children, we were mermaids," *Entropy*, Spring 2020
"Exhibit A," *Honey + Lime*, Spring 2020
"Isopod," *FEED*, Summer 2020
"Florida Girl," *Whale Road Review*, Summer 2020
"Near miss" and "We have nearly run out of helium," *Saltfront*, Fall 2020
"Walk it back," *Minnow*, Fall 2020
"Transfusion, *Floresta*, January 2021

"Home," *The Curator*, March 2021

"Easement," and "What wolves have you been?," *Anti-Heroin Chic*, December 2021

"Weighted.," *Blue House Journal*, Winter 2022

"Home," *Thimble*, Spring 2022

"Firefly," "The Beekeepers," "She Fakes an Injury to Save Her Children," "Fossils in Flagrante Delicto: A poem for Prehistoric Turtles," are all included in the chapbook, *As Wild Animals*, published by Dancing Girl Press, Fall 2012

"Insufficient Funds," "The portrait of an addict as the elements," "When we were children, we were mermaids.," "Florida Girl," "Things no one told my parents and, also, why I got a D in geography," "At The Party," "Every poem is about my father," "The Fire-Eater," "Leaving," "Exterminator," "Homecoming," "Hurricane," "My Father's Hands," "Close," "Broken Water," "Some Men Bring Flowers," "Emergency Procedures," "Recovering," "Everything," are all included in the chapbook, *Running Aground*, Finishing Line Press, Fall 2020

Debts I can't repay:

Many of these poems began germinating years ago, during my time at Pacific University, and I will forever be grateful for everything I learned there & my fellow students and amazing faculty. The Young Chicago Author's Writing Teacher's Collective has been a continual source of inspiration and support, both as a writer and educator. My first readers and five a.m. texters and co-conspirators, Jessica and Amanda. My parents for always. Maya, Hermes, and Kuma, who couldn't care less that I named them here. Everything I've ever read. Every small animal that crosses my path and pauses long enough for me to recognize it. And Jason, for keeping our four walls standing, and for knowing when we need to break out of them.

About the Author

Elizabeth Joy Levinson is a high school teacher in Chicago, where she lives with her husband & pets. She has an MFA from Pacific University and an MAT in Biology from Miami University. She is the author of two chapbooks, As Wild Animals (Dancing Girl Press) and Running Aground (Finishing Line Press) and has had work published in many independent journals.

About the Press

Unsolicited Press is based out of Portland, Oregon and focuses on the works of the unsung and underrepresented. As a womxn-owned, all-volunteer small publisher that doesn't worry about profits as much as championing exceptional literature, we have the privilege of partnering with authors skirting the fringes of the lit world. We've worked with emerging and award-winning authors such as Shann Ray, Amy Shimshon-Santo, Brook Bhagat, Kris Amos, and John W. Bateman.

Learn more at unsolicitedpress.com. Find us on twitter and instagram.